"Children and adults will love these gentle, empowering books. The Learning to Get Along series is a powerful tool for teaching children essential social skills such as empathy, respect, cooperation, and kindness. This straightforward and insightful series helps children visualize how their appropriate behavior positively impacts themselves and others. I heartily recommend this as a solid, classic resource for teaching affective skills to young children."

—**Dr. Stephen R. Covey, Author,** *The 7 Habits of Highly Effective People*

Be Polite and Kind

Cheri J. Meiners, M.Ed.
Illustrated by Meredith Johnson

free spirit
PUBLISHING®

Helping kids
help themselves™
since 1983

Library of Congress Cataloging-in-Publication Data
Meiners, Cheri J., 1957–
    Be polite and kind / Cheri J. Meiners ; illustrations by Meredith Johnson.
        p. cm. — (Learning to get along)
Summary: Demonstrates ways of showing politeness, speaking kindly, using basic courtesies, and respecting the feelings of others. Includes role-playing activities.
    ISBN 1-57542-151-8
 1. Courtesy—Juvenile literature. 2. Kindness—Juvenile literature. 3. Conduct of life—Juvenile literature. [1. Etiquette. 2. Conduct of life.] I. Johnson, Meredith, ill. II. Title.
BJ1533.C9M45 2003
177'.1—dc22

                                                                2003019873

Cover and interior design by Marieka Heinlen
Edited by Marjorie Lisovskis

10 9 8 7 6 5 4 3
Printed in Hong Kong

Free Spirit Publishing Inc.
217 Fifth Avenue North, Suite 200
Minneapolis, MN 55401-1299
(612) 338-2068
help4kids@freespirit.com
www.freespirit.com

Dedication

To James, whose kind
words reflect a
generous heart

Acknowledgments

I wish to thank Meredith Johnson for her beautiful illustrations. I also thank Judy Galbraith and all those at Free Spirit who believed in this series. Special thanks go to Marieka Heinlen for the lovely design and to Margie Lisovskis who, as editor, has contributed her wonderful expertise and creativity. Finally, I am grateful to Mary Jane Weiss, Ph.D., whose insight, skill, and caring have done much to advance the field of teaching social skills.

I talk with people every day.

My words can show others that they are important to me.

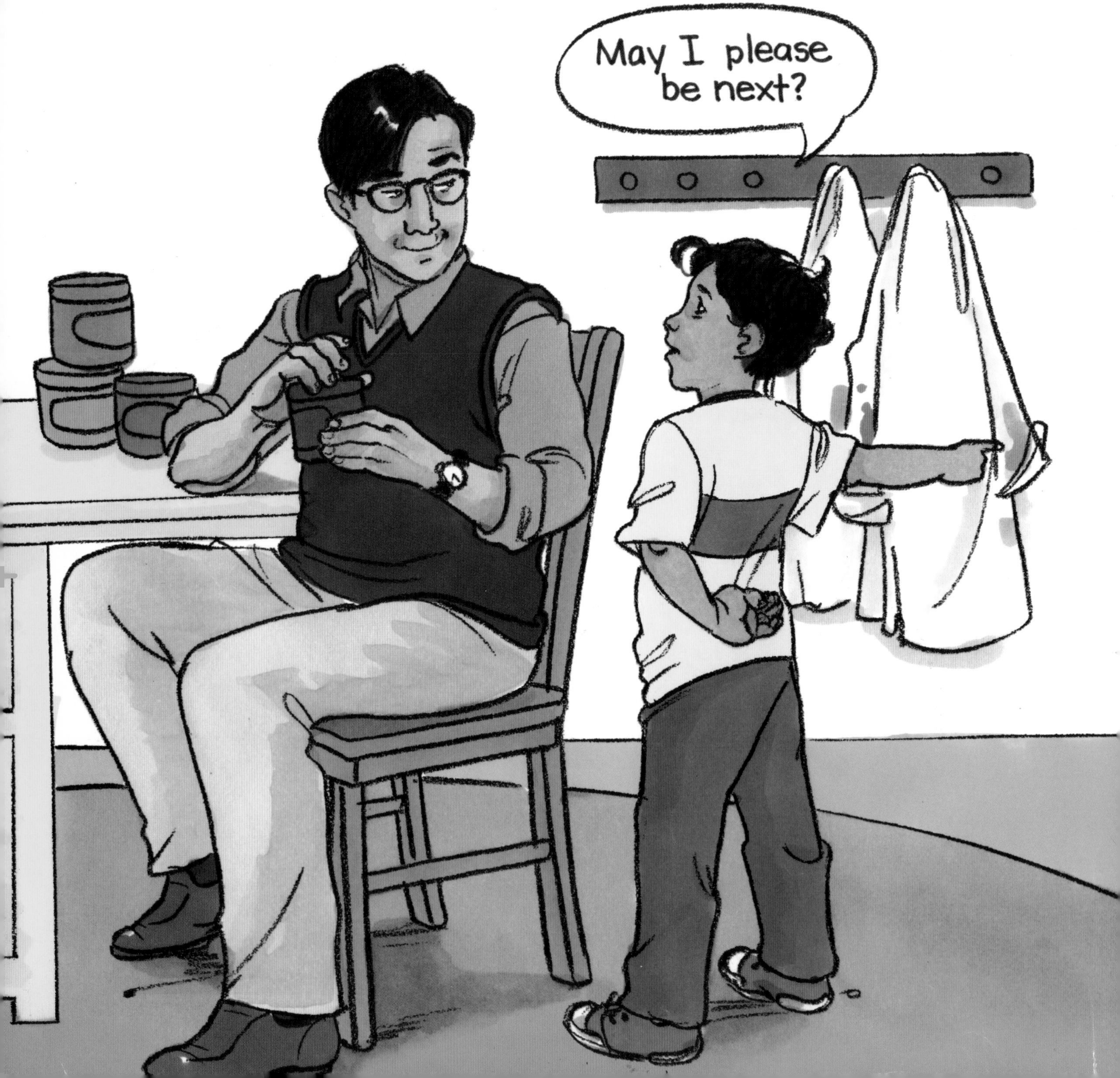
May I please be next?

I say "Please" when I ask for something.

And I say "Please" when I ask for help.

If I ask in a polite way, the person will probably want to help me.

When someone says something nice or does something for me, I say "Thank you."

I can notice all the kind things people do.

Another time I say "Thank you" is when someone gives me something.

I smile and show I'm glad that the person thought about me.

If the person is somewhere else,
I can send a note or say "Thank you"
on the phone.

I can show that I appreciate the kind things others do.

There are many times
when I can help someone.

If the person thanks me, I can smile and say "You're welcome."

When I yawn, cough, or sneeze,

I say "Excuse me."

I also say "Excuse me"

when I do something that could bother someone.

When I do something by accident,

I say "I'm sorry."

I like to say kind things.

I can notice when someone is friendly
or helpful or does a good job.

I can think before I say something.

I can be polite and kind
when I say what I think and feel.

I know polite things to say.

When I use words to help someone feel good, I show respect.

When I speak polite words in a kind way, people enjoy being around me.

It helps us get along.

I want people to treat me with respect,

so that's how I treat them.

Ways to Reinforce the Ideas in *Be Polite and Kind*

As you read each page spread, ask children:

- What's happening in this picture?
- Who's being polite (kind)? How can you tell?

Here are additional questions you might discuss:

Pages 1–3

- Who do you talk with every day?
- How do you show other people they are important to you? What do you do? What do you say?

Pages 4–25

- When are some times that you say "Thank you" ("You're welcome," "Excuse me," "I'm sorry")?
- What does it mean to be polite (kind)? How does it feel when someone says polite (kind) words to you? Why?
- How does it feel when someone is *not* polite (kind)?

Pages 26–27

- What is respect? *(You might explain respect by saying, "When you show respect to people, you show that you think they are important. Being polite and kind shows respect. It feels good to be treated with respect.")*
- *(Read and point to each polite phrase)* When do you say (ask) this? What are some other ways to say (ask) it?

  Note: The boy and his sister are speaking in American Sign Language (ASL). The girl is saying "Thank you"; the boy is saying "You're welcome." The activity on pages 33–34 teaches how to sign some polite phrases.

Pages 28–31

- Why is it important to be polite and kind?

Politeness Games

Read this book often with your child or group of children. Once children are familiar with the book, refer to it when teachable moments arise involving manners, kindness, and respect. Make it a point to notice and comment when children's words and actions are courteous and thoughtful. In addition, use the activities on pages 33–35 to reinforce children's understanding of how to be polite and kind. Most of the activities refer to these words and scenarios:

| Please. | You're welcome. | I'm sorry. | Hello. |
| Thank you. | Excuse me. | May I? | Good job! |

Sample Scenarios:

- At school, Vivek asks to go to the bathroom.
- Katie's teacher said she likes what Katie wrote.
- Sarah's mom gave Sarah a snack.
- The sitter thanked Zach for helping set the table.

- When Andrea's friend was talking, Andrea yawned.
- A friend told Erika, "I like your shirt."
- At home, Damani wants to play with his sister's stuffed animal.

- Joseph's dad put a bandage on Joseph's knee.
- James opened the door when someone knocked. It was his friend.
- While walking in a line, Ka bumped into someone.

What Do You Say?

Level 1

Read aloud one of the sample scenarios (or make up your own). Ask: "What can this person say?" (As a prompt, you may want to display the respectful words on a board or poster and refer to them.)

Level 2

Preparation: Give children three index cards apiece and have them write a different phrase (respectful words) on each card.

Read aloud one of the scenarios. Say: "Imagine you are (name of person in scenario). What do you say? If one of your cards has a good answer, raise your hand." Invite children to read their appropriate words.

Beanbag Toss

Preparation: Use one beanbag and the scenarios. Before the game, you may want to think of additional scenarios or invite children to suggest some. Write these down for your own reference.

Level 1

Explain that you will tell a short story, ask a question, and toss the beanbag to someone. Children are to remain quiet so the child with the beanbag can respond. Assure children that everyone will get a turn. Read a scenario and ask: "What can (name of person) say?" Throw the beanbag to a child. The child responds. Read the next scenario; then have the child throw the beanbag to someone else to answer. If a child does not answer correctly, discuss the appropriate response and then give the child another chance with a new scenario.

Level 2

Follow the steps in Level 1, but instead of reading scenarios to children, have them think of their own scenarios as they play.

Manners Signing

Teach children how to use American Sign Language (ASL) to sign the following respectful words:

"Yes"	"No"	"Please"	"Thank you"	"You're welcome"	"I'm sorry"
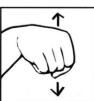	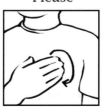				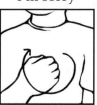

Ask children to identify what the two children on pages 26 and 27 are saying (signing). If you wish, invite children to use sign language at other times during the activities, such as in response to "What Do You Say?" on page 33.

Manners Spinners

Materials: Large paper plate, metal fastener (brad), cardstock, scissors, marker; index cards and bag to hold the cards

Preparation: With a marker, divide the plate into eight wedges and write each of the respectful phrases from page 32 in a different wedge. Use the cardstock to make a spinner and fasten it to the plate with the brad. Write scenarios on the index cards and place the cards in the bag.

Invite a child to draw a scenario card from the bag. Read or have the child read the scenario and ask: "What can this child say?" Then have the same child (or another child) answer by pointing the spinner to a correct answer. Help nonreaders as needed, and continue play so that all children have a chance to draw scenarios and choose polite words.

Variation: Help, or have, children make and color their own individual spinners. Have all children point their spinners to respectful phrases and then hold up and compare their choices.

Manners Game Show

Materials: 8½" x 11" paper, marker, construction paper, whiteboard or bulletin board and magnets, tape, or pushpins

Preparation: Write individual scenarios on sheets of paper and mount them on the board in a grid formation. Number sheets of construction paper and cover each scenario with a numbered sheet, attached at the top.

Level 1

Have two or three children sit in chairs near the board; other children can be the audience. Call on one of the players to choose a number. Lift the numbered flap, read the scenario, and ask the player: "What can this person say?" If the child answers appropriately, everyone applauds. If not, ask the next player. After each player has a turn to answer correctly, rotate players.

Level 2

Have each child in the group write one or more scenarios for the game, putting a correct respectful phrase on the back of the scenario page. Mount the scenarios and play as in Level 1.

Who Has Good Manners?

Materials: Cards and bag prepared for "Manners Spinners" activity (see above)

Have three children draw a scenario card from a bag and quietly decide which child will give an appropriate respectful response. The other two children think of different (inappropriate) answers. Read the scenario aloud and have each of the three children give their response. Ask the rest of the group: "Who has good manners?" Discuss children's ideas, and continue the game with a new threesome.

Manners Board Game

Materials: Sheet of cardstock at least 18" x 18", ruler, marker; index cards, one standard die, game tokens (such as buttons in various colors and sizes, one per player)

Preparation: With the marker, draw a 3-inch border around the perimeter of the cardstock. Fill in lines every 3 inches to make 20 squares. On two adjacent squares, write "Home" and "School." Write different scenarios on ten random spaces. On the eight remaining spaces, write places, such as: "Lunch Table," "Friend's Home," "Movie Theater," "Playground," "Ball Game," "Car or Bus," "Store," and "Library." Tailor the places to fit your group of children. Then, on index cards, write respectful phrases so you have a deck of 16–20 cards with each phrase written on two cards. Shuffle and place the cards in a pile facedown in the middle of the game board.

Starting at "Home" on the board, a child rolls the die and moves her or his token forward the correct number of spaces. If the token lands on a scenario, read the situation and have the player respond with respectful words. If the token lands on a place, have the player draw a card from the middle and tell how the respectful words on the card could be used in that setting. (For instance, with "Movie Theater" and "May I?" a child could say, "May I please get some popcorn?") If needed, offer an example or two to prompt the child. The player then places the card at the bottom of the deck and play continues. The game ends when all players arrive at "School."

Courtesy Role Plays

Help children role-play the following examples using best manners. If you wish, use dolls, action figures, or stuffed animals for some or all of the role plays.

- **Mealtime:** Role-play serving and passing food. Focus on "Please" and "Thank you," on chewing with lips closed, and on waiting to speak until all food is swallowed. This could culminate in writing invitations to guests to join children for a special meal.
- **Telephone:** Using play phones, role-play calling someone and answering the phone, using phrases such as: "Hello, this is Carla. May I please speak with Tranh?" "This is Tranh. How are you, Carla?" or "Just a minute please."
- **Friends at the door:** Role-play greetings and leave-taking, with the host thanking the visitor for coming and the visitor thanking the host for having him or her as a guest.
- **A party:** Practice welcoming guests, thanking them for any gifts, sharing toys, and using mealtime and door manners.
- **Bus or car pool:** Role-play greeting the driver, using seatbelts, sitting and talking quietly, and thanking the driver for the ride.
- **At play or sports:** Role-play including all who wish to play, taking turns, and giving encouragement to other players.

Variation: With each situation, tell examples of good and poor manners. Then ask questions such as: "Is this polite?" "Is this good manners?" "Does this show respect?" "Is this kind?" Have children give each example a thumbs-up or thumbs-down. For thumbs-down, ask: "What could this person say (do) instead?" or "What is a better way?"

More titles in Free Spirit's Learning to Get Along® series:

Our Learning to Get Along series by Cheri J. Meiners, M.Ed., helps children learn, understand, and practice basic social and emotional skills. Real-life situations, lots of diversity, and concrete examples make these read-aloud books appropriate for childcare settings, schools, and the home. Each book focuses on a specific skill and ends with ideas for reinforcing what the children have learned. *Each book: $10.95, 40 pp., color illust., S/C, 9" x 9", ages 4–8.*

KNOW AND FOLLOW RULES
Shows children that following rules can help us stay safe, learn, be fair, get along, and instill a positive sense of pride.

RESPECT AND TAKE CARE OF THINGS
Children learn to put things where they belong and ask permission to use things. Teaches simple environmental awareness.

TRY AND STICK WITH IT
Introduces children to flexibilty, stick-to-it-iveness (perseverance), and the benefits of trying something new.

TALK AND WORK IT OUT
Peaceful conflict resolution is simplified so children can learn to calm down, state the problem, listen, and think of and try solutions.

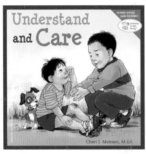

UNDERSTAND AND CARE
Builds empathy in children; guides them to show they care by listening to others and respecting their feelings.

SHARE AND TAKE TURNS
Gives reasons to share; describes four ways to share; points out that children can also share their knowledge, creativity, and time.

JOIN IN AND PLAY
Teaches the basics of cooperation, getting along, making friends, and being a friend.

WHEN I FEEL AFRAID
Helps children understand their fears; teaches simple coping skills; encourages children to talk with trusted adults about their fears.

LISTEN AND LEARN
Introduces and explains what listening means, why it's important to listen, and how to listen well.

To place an order or to request a free catalog of SELF-HELP FOR KIDS®
and SELF-HELP FOR TEENS® materials, please write, call, email, or visit our Web site:

Free Spirit Publishing Inc.
217 Fifth Avenue North • Suite 200 • Minneapolis, MN 55401 • toll-free 800.735.7323 • local 612.338.2068
fax 612.337.5050 • help4kids@freespirit.com • www.freespirit.com